from SEA TO SHINING SEA

NEW YORK

By Dennis Brindell Fradin

CONSULTANTS

Wendell Tripp, Ph.D., Editor *New York History;*
New York State Historical Association, Cooperstown

Robert L. Hillerich, Ph.D., Professor Emeritus, Bowling Green State University;
Consultant, Pinellas County Schools, Florida

CHILDRENS PRESS®
CHICAGO

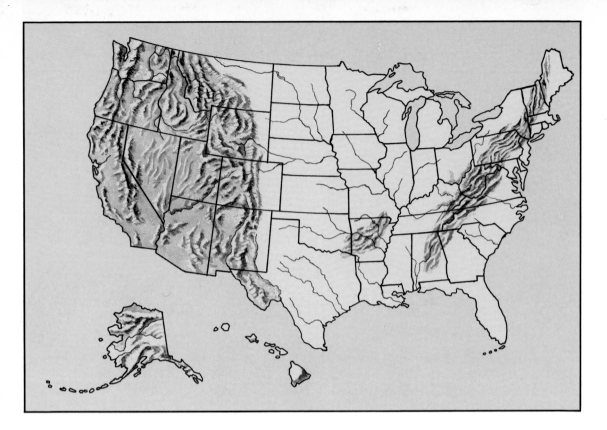

New York is one of the three Middle Atlantic states. The other Middle Atlantic states are New Jersey and Pennsylvania.

For June Rachuy Brindel—aunt, author, and inspiration

Front cover picture, New York City at dusk; page 1, tourists on Liberty Island; back cover, Whiteface Mountain, in the Adirondacks north of Lake Placid

Project Editor: Joan Downing
Design Director: Karen Kohn
Research Assistant: Judith Bloom Fradin
Typesetting: Graphic Connections, Inc.
Engraving: Liberty Photoengraving

Library of Congress Cataloging-in-Publication Data

Fradin, Dennis B.
  New York / by Dennis Brindell Fradin.
    p.   cm. — (From sea to shining sea)
  Includes index.
  Summary: An overview of the Empire State, introducing its history, geography, industries, sites of interest, and famous people.
  ISBN 0-516-03832-X
  1. New York (State)—Juvenile literature. [1. New York (State).] I. Title. II. Series: Fradin, Dennis B. From sea to shining sea.
F119.3.F67   1993   93-10334
974.7—dc20   CIP
                                                   AC

Table of Contents

A Coney Island merry-go-round

Introducing the Empire State

New York is in the northeastern United States. The Dutch built its first settlements. Then, England ruled New York for more than 100 years. In 1788, New York became one of the thirteen original states.

George Washington understood New York's importance. He said that New York would become the center of an American empire. New York is nicknamed the "Empire State."

Washington's words came true. The Empire State leads the country at making books and clothing. It is a big producer of apples and milk. New York also has the country's largest city. This is New York City. It is home to the Statue of Liberty.

Much more is special about New York. Where is Niagara Falls? Where were two presidents named Roosevelt born? Where do the Yankees and Mets play baseball? Where do the Knicks play basketball? Where was the first black woman in Congress born?

Overleaf: Horseshoe Lake, Adirondack Park

A picture map of New York

Where was the author of *The Wizard of Oz* born? The answer to these questions is: the Empire State!

Mountains, Rivers, and Lakes

MOUNTAINS, RIVERS, AND LAKES

Lakes Erie and Ontario are two of the five Great Lakes. The others are Lakes Huron, Michigan, and Superior.

Sunset over Great South Bay near Amityville, Long Island

New York is one of the Middle Atlantic states. On a map, it looks like a low-topped boot. To the southeast, the Atlantic Ocean splashes against the boot's heel. New Jersey and Pennsylvania lie to the south. Part of Pennsylvania and Ontario, Canada, are to the west. So are Lakes Erie and Ontario. To the north is Quebec, Canada. Vermont, Massachusetts, and Connecticut form New York's eastern border.

New York covers 49,108 square miles. Most of this land is hills or mountains. The Adirondack Mountains are in northeastern New York. Mount Marcy is in the Adirondacks. The state's tallest peak, it is 5,344 feet high. South of the Adirondacks are the Catskill Mountains. New York also has some low flatlands. These flatlands lie along the state's large bodies of water: the Atlantic Ocean, Hudson River, and Lakes Erie, Ontario, and Champlain.

WATERS, WOODS, AND WILDLIFE

The Hudson River is New York's longest river. It begins on Mount Marcy and flows 300 miles. The

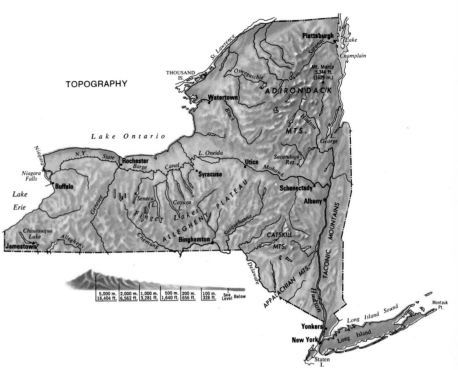

TOPOGRAPHY

Hudson empties into the ocean at New York City. The Mohawk, Delaware, Susquehanna, and Genesee are other important New York rivers. The St. Lawrence River forms the state's northwest border with Canada. The Niagara River separates New York from Canada on the west.

New York has thousands of lakes. Lakes Ontario, Erie, and Champlain form part of its border. Oneida Lake is the biggest lake completely inside the state. It is in the middle of New York. West of Oneida Lake are the eleven Finger Lakes. The largest of them are Cayuga and Seneca lakes.

Left: Adirondack Park, in the Adirondacks

The Finger Lakes get that name from their long, slender shapes.

9

Porcupines are among the animals that live in New York.

Farm country in the south-central part of the state

Half of New York is wooded. The sugar maple is New York's state tree. Oaks, birches, and pines also grow in New York's woods.

Deer and bears live in New York. So do woodchucks, raccoons, beavers, rabbits, foxes, and opossums. The bluebird is the state bird. Woodpeckers drill holes in New York's trees. Geese, ducks, and wild turkeys also are seen about the state.

CLIMATE

The Great Lakes, mountains, and ocean give New York different kinds of weather. Syracuse, Rochester,

and Buffalo receive more than 100 inches of snow a year. Nighttime winter temperatures in the mountains and some other areas can dip below 0 degrees Fahrenheit. New York City's January temperatures are around 30 degrees Fahrenheit.

Summer temperatures in New York City are about 75 degrees Fahrenheit. In the Adirondack Mountains, summer temperatures are around 66 degrees Fahrenheit.

Now and then, a hurricane slams into New York's coast. One of these huge storms hit Long Island in 1938. The island actually shook. About 600 people died in that hurricane.

A winter scene on the West Branch of Cazenovia Creek

From Ancient Times Until Today

FROM ANCIENT TIMES UNTIL TODAY

About 2 million years ago, the Ice Age began. Nearly all of New York was covered by glaciers. These ice sheets were up to 2 miles thick. As they moved, the glaciers spread rich soil over New York. They also deepened valleys. Later, the valleys filled with water and became lakes.

Mastodons and mammoths roamed New York during the Ice Age. They were related to today's elephants. A mastodon tusk was once found in New York City. Mastodons and mammoths died out about 10,000 years ago. The Ice Age was ending at that time.

AMERICAN INDIANS

Ancient Indians reached New York more than 11,000 years ago. They hunted animals with spears. Some of their spear points and tools have been found.

By the year 1300, Iroquois Indians lived in New York. They were called the "People of the Longhouse." The Iroquois lived in long wooden

Opposite page: The Statue of Liberty

13

houses. There were five groups of Iroquois. They were the Mohawk, Oneida, Onondaga, Cayuga, and Seneca.

At first, the Iroquois fought one another. Around the year 1570, they made peace. They formed the Iroquois Federation. A village near what is now Syracuse became its capital. There, leaders from all five groups met in a special longhouse. The Iroquois worked together. They became more powerful than any other Indian group.

Several groups of Algonquian-speaking Indians also lived in New York. The Delaware were known as peacemakers. They settled disputes between other groups. The Wappinger, Mahican, Munsee, and Montauk tribes were other Algonquians.

EUROPEAN EXPLORERS

Giovanni da Verrazano was the first European to explore New York. He was Italian, but he worked for France. In 1524, Verrazano entered New York's harbor. A group of Algonquians welcomed him.

France had built settlements in Canada in the early 1600s. In 1609, Samuel de Champlain came down from Canada. He explored around the large lake in northeastern New York. Champlain named

the lake for himself. He claimed the land for France.

Henry Hudson, an English explorer, also arrived in 1609. He worked for the Netherlands. Hudson sailed the *Half Moon* up a great river. Later, the river was named for him.

Henry Hudson was hired by the Dutch (above) to find a shorter route to Asia. Instead, he found New York and sailed up what is now the Hudson River.

DUTCH AND ENGLISH RULE

Based partly on Hudson's work, the Dutch claimed New Netherland. It included parts of New York, New Jersey, Connecticut, and Delaware. Dutch people soon sailed to New Netherland to live.

The Dutch founded Fort Orange in 1624. It was New York's first European-built town. In 1625,

The Dutch are the people who live in the Netherlands.

15

the Dutch began laying out New Amsterdam. It was on Manhattan Island. The Dutch lived along the Hudson River. They built towns and farms between Fort Orange and New Amsterdam. By 1660, only 5,000 colonists lived in present-day New York State. Some were English, Irish, and German people.

By 1660, England also had colonies along the Atlantic Coast. England added New Netherland to its holdings in 1664. English warships forced the Dutch to give up control of New Netherland.

The English renamed New Netherland. It became New York. It was named for James, the English Duke of York and Albany. New Amsterdam

Below: The Dutch surrendered New Amsterdam to the English in 1664.

became New York City. Fort Orange became Albany.

Growth continued to be slow under English rule. By 1700, the colony's population was only 20,000. Most of the people lived between Schenectady and New York City. Many lived on Long Island.

Meanwhile, England and France were at war. Both countries wanted to rule North America. Between 1689 and 1763, they fought four wars. Many Indians helped France. Much of the fighting took place in New York. In 1690, French and Indians attacked Schenectady. More than sixty colonists were killed.

The fourth war (1754-1763) was called the French and Indian War. During that war, Robert Rogers led a group of fighting men. They were called Rogers' Rangers. The rangers helped England capture Forts Niagara, Ticonderoga, and Crown Point. England finally defeated France in 1763.

A French and Indian War encampment is re-created at Old Fort Niagara.

THE REVOLUTIONARY WAR

The wars had cost England much money. To pay for the wars, England began taxing the American colonists. The Americans rebelled against the taxes.

A man dressed as a Revolutionary War soldier stands by a cannon at Fort Stanwyx National Monument in Rome, New York.

In 1775, they began fighting the Revolutionary War. The Americans wanted to form their own country, the United States.

About 100 Revolutionary War battles took place in New York. In 1776, Nathan Hale became a spy for General George Washington. The twenty-one-year-old Connecticut teacher was captured on Long Island. Before he was hanged, Hale said: "I only regret that I have but one life to lose for my country."

In November 1776, a battle was fought at Fort Washington. Today, this is part of New York City. Margaret Corbin fired a cannon at the English in this battle. She was one of the first women to fight for American independence.

The English captured New York City. But the Americans did better elsewhere in New York. In 1777, they won battles at Oriskany and Saratoga. The war ended in 1781. A peace treaty was signed in 1783. On November 25, 1783, the English finally evacuated (left) New York City. For many years, November 25 was a New York holiday. New Yorkers called it Evacuation Day.

Growth of the Eleventh State

American leaders wrote the United States Constitution in 1787. It created the country's government. New York approved the Constitution on July 26, 1788. By doing that, it became the eleventh state.

New York City was the United States capital from 1785 to 1790. In 1789, George Washington became the first president of the United States. He took the oath of office at Federal Hall on Wall Street.

In the early 1800s, settlers moved to western New York. Buffalo was begun in 1803. Rochester was settled in 1812. Some people headed even far-

George Washington taking the oath in 1789 as the first President of the United States

ther west. They moved to lands like Illinois and Michigan. These places were on the Great Lakes.

Between 1817 and 1825, the Erie Canal was dug across New York. It ran from Albany to Buffalo. The canal connected the Hudson River and Atlantic Ocean with the Great Lakes. Western farmers could then ship their crops to New York City. New Yorkers could send their goods out west. Boats carried crops and goods across the Great Lakes. Then they went along the Erie Canal and Hudson River to New York City. Buffalo, Rochester, Schenectady, and other cities along the canal grew.

New York's first railroad began running in 1831. It connected Albany with Schenectady. Other railroads linked southern New York cities with New York City.

By 1850, New York had 3,097,394 people. That was more people than any other state. Many of them had just come from Ireland and Germany.

FIGHTS AGAINST SLAVERY AND FOR WOMEN'S RIGHTS

All thirteen colonies had allowed slavery. In the late 1700s, northern states started ending slavery. New York outlawed slavery in 1827.

The first railroad in the state began running in 1831.

In 1827, John Russwurm and Samuel Cornish founded *Freedom's Journal*. This was an antislavery newspaper in New York City. It was the country's first black-run paper. In 1847, Frederick Douglass began an antislavery paper in Rochester. It was called the *North Star*. Douglass was a great black leader.

Isabella Baumfree spoke against slavery. She was the first black woman to do so. Baumfree was born in Ulster County, New York. She called herself Sojourner Truth. She traveled around the country calling for an end to slavery.

New Yorkers also hid southern slaves who were escaping to Canada. Douglass's Rochester home was such a hiding place. So was the Michigan

Sojourner Truth (left) and Frederick Douglass (right) both spoke out against slavery.

Avenue Baptist Church in Buffalo. The network of hiding places was called the Underground Railroad.

White women also spoke out against slavery. Then they began working for women's rights. New Yorker Elizabeth Cady Stanton was one of their leaders. She organized the first women's rights convention. It was held in Seneca Falls in 1848.

In 1861, the Civil War started. It was fought between the northern states (the Union) and the southern states (the Confederacy). One reason for the war was slavery. Nearly 500,000 New Yorkers served the Union. This amounted to nearly one-fourth of the northern forces. The North won the war in 1865. The country's remaining slaves were freed that year.

NEW STRUCTURES AND INDUSTRIES

After the Civil War, much building took place in New York City. John Roebling began the Brooklyn Bridge in 1869. He died before it was finished. His son, Washington Roebling, finished the famous bridge in 1883. That bridge connects Brooklyn with the tip of Manhattan.

In 1884, France gave the United States the Statue of Liberty. This huge statue was placed in

About 50,000 New Yorkers died in the Civil War.

The Civil War Monument in Grand Army Plaza, Brooklyn

New York Harbor in 1886. It became a symbol of the United States. It stands for freedom. Millions of Europeans saw the statue when they entered the country. They came from Italy, Greece, Poland, and other lands.

Many of these people got jobs in New York's factories. They made clothing, books, glassware, and other items. Other workers built New York City's tall buildings. In 1853, Elisha Otis of Yonkers invented the electric elevator. Elevators moved people and goods up and down in the new buildings.

In 1888, George Eastman of Rochester invented the Kodak camera. The Eastman Kodak

The Brooklyn Bridge was finished in 1883.

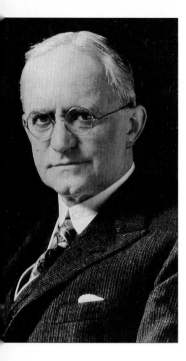

George Eastman

During the Great Depression, people who were out of work often stood in welfare lines to get food.

Company became a giant name in photography. Eastman's company helped Rochester grow.

By 1880, New York had over 5 million people. By 1910, its population was over 9 million.

TWO WORLD WARS AND THE GREAT DEPRESSION

In 1917, the United States entered World War I (1914-1918). New York provided more soldiers than any other state. More than 500,000 New Yorkers helped win World War I.

In 1929, the Great Depression hit the country. Banks closed. Companies went out of business. People lost their jobs. These hard times lasted ten years.

Americans turned to Franklin Delano Roosevelt (FDR). He was the governor of New York. In

1932, Americans elected him president of the United States. He held that office longer than any other president (1933-1945). His programs were called the New Deal. They put many people back to work.

In 1933, FDR named Frances Perkins secretary of labor. She had worked for him in New York. Perkins was the first woman appointed to the cabinet. She helped American workers.

FDR also led the United States through World War II (1939-1945). The United States entered this war in 1941. New York's factories made goods for the war effort. Once again, New York sent the most people to serve. More than 1.6 million New York men and women were in uniform. About 31,000 of them died helping win the war.

World War II ended in 1945. In that year, world leaders formed the United Nations (UN). This organization is based in New York. It works to keep peace. Nearly every country is a member.

NEW YORK FACES THE FUTURE

New York faces the year 2000 with problems. Pollution is one of its worst problems. New York's ground, air, and water have been badly polluted.

Frances Perkins helped set up the Social Security system. It provides income to retired people.

A World War II bomber at the Genesee County Air Museum

Families were moved from Love Canal in 1978. That is a neighborhood in Niagara Falls. Chemicals dumped there were making people sick.

Many New York factories send harmful smoke into the air. People breathe these poisons. Even the rain over New York can be harmful. Pollution turns it into acid rain. Trees in the Adirondacks are being killed by this rain.

The Hudson River has also been damaged. Wastes from farms and cities have been dumped into it. People cannot eat Hudson River fish. They contain poisons. Yet, some cities' drinking water comes from the Hudson. John Cronin moves up and down the Hudson in a small boat. He stops cities and companies from polluting the river.

The "Toxic Avengers" are also fighting pollution. They are New York City teenagers who fight chemical dumping. State and city officials are working to improve New York, too. A 1992 program will cut down on air pollution from cars.

New York City also has some huge "people problems." Many people in the city are very poor. About 75,000 are homeless. The city also has a high crime rate. Each year about 2,000 people are murdered there. The city has the country's highest death rate from AIDS.

In 1989, David Dinkins was elected mayor of New York City. He became the first black mayor of the country's largest city. Dinkins is working to make life better there.

The Empire State's leaders are also dealing with these problems. What they do is important to New Yorkers and to all Americans. In many ways, New York helps decide the country's course.

Crowds of people on New York City's Fifth Avenue

Overleaf: Students attending a lecture at Barnard College

27

New Yorkers and Their Work

NEW YORKERS AND THEIR WORK

T he 1990 United States Census counted 17,990,455 New Yorkers. Only California had more people. Three-fourths of all New Yorkers are white. Many of them have German, Italian, Irish, English, or Polish backgrounds. Nearly 3 million New Yorkers are black. Another 2.2 million are Hispanic. Their families came from Puerto Rico, Mexico, and other Spanish-speaking lands.

Lately, Asians have been New York's fastest-growing group. There are about 700,000 Asian New Yorkers. New York is also home to more than 60,000 American Indians. Many are Seneca, Oneida, Mohawk, Onondaga, Tuscarora, or Cayuga.

People of every faith live in New York. Over one-sixth of the country's Jewish people are New Yorkers.

People of nearly every race and national background live in New York.

NEW YORKERS AT WORK

Over 8 million New Yorkers have jobs. They produce goods and services worth $500 billion a year. Few countries can match that figure.

This architecture student attends Rensselaer Polytechnic Institute in Troy. Rensselaer is one of the state's many private colleges and universities.

This worker at the Corning Glass Works is making a piece of famous Steuben glass.

About 2.5 million New Yorkers do service work. Nurses, doctors, and lawyers are counted as service workers. So are people in advertising. New York City's Madison Avenue companies make many advertisements. They are seen around the country.

Nearly 2 million New Yorkers sell goods. Some well-known stores have their headquarters in the state. The F. W. Woolworth stores are based in New York City.

Government work employs 1.5 million New Yorkers. Many of them are teachers. New York City has the country's largest public school system. About 1 million students attend the city's public schools. The state also has the country's biggest public college system. It is called the State University of New York. More than 200,000 students attend its many branches.

Almost 800,000 New Yorkers work in banking. Most of the country's largest banks are in New York City. One is Citibank. That is North America's biggest bank. The country's biggest stock exchange is on New York City's Wall Street. It is the New York Stock Exchange.

Over 1 million New Yorkers make products. Printed goods such as books and magazines lead the list of products. The state also ranks first in making

clothing and jewelry. Cameras, office machines, glass, and paints are other important products.

Over 100,000 New Yorkers live on farms. Milk is the state's top farm product. Only Wisconsin and California produce more milk than New York. Only Vermont produces more maple syrup. The state is a leading grower of apples, cherries, grapes, pears, snap beans, lettuce, sweet corn, cabbage, and onions. Wine is also produced in New York.

About 6,000 New Yorkers are miners. They mine garnet, salt, and lead. Limestone and sand and gravel are also important.

In addition, New York is a major fishing state. Perch, walleyes, and bullheads come from Lakes Erie and Ontario. Lobster, oysters, and clams are leading ocean catches.

More than 100,000 people live and work on farms in New York.

Overleaf: The George Eastman House and Museum, in Rochester

A Tour of the Empire State

A Tour of the Empire State

*E*ach year, about 25 million people visit New York. They go to the Statue of Liberty and Niagara Falls. They also explore the state's cities, mountains, and forests.

New York City and Long Island

Only nine of the fifty states have more people than New York City.

Grand Central Station

New York City lies along the ocean in southeastern New York. It's the country's largest city. About 7.3 million people live there. No other United States city is even half that big. The city has five boroughs. They are Manhattan, the Bronx, Queens, Brooklyn, and Staten Island. Brooklyn and Queens are on the west end of Long Island. People travel between the boroughs by highways and subway trains. They also use ferryboats, tunnels, and bridges.

New York City is called the "Big Apple." Jazz musicians of the 1920s gave it that nickname. They meant that playing in New York City was the big time.

The Big Apple has many of the biggest or busiest places. The city has the country's busiest subway system. About 4 million people ride it daily. Grand

34

Central Station is the world's biggest railroad station. The World Trade Center is the world's largest office center. The Metropolitan Museum of Art is the biggest United States art museum. Nearby is the country's biggest science museum. That is the American Museum of Natural History.

Sports fans watch the city's many pro teams. The Yankees and Mets are the baseball teams. The Yankees have won twenty-two World Series. The Mets have won it twice. The Knicks are the city's basketball team. The Rangers and Islanders are the hockey teams. The Islanders won the Stanley Cup four years in a row (1980-1983). The Jets and

The Brooklyn Bridge connects Brooklyn to Manhattan Island and New York City.

The Mets play ball in Shea Stadium.

Giants are the football teams. But they play in New Jersey.

Playgoers enjoy the many plays in the city's Broadway area. Ballet and opera lovers attend performances at Lincoln Center. Carnegie Hall hosts many concerts by well-known musicians. The Whitney and Guggenheim museums attract modern art fans. So does the Museum of Modern Art.

The 102-story Empire State Building is a well-known landmark. It opened in 1931. Then, it was the world's tallest building. Visitors still tour the building. They take elevators to the top floor. From there, they can see up to 50 miles away.

Left: The Empire State Building
Right: The American Museum of Natural History

The Statue of Liberty is a favorite stop for visitors. The statue is on Liberty Island, off the tip of Manhattan. Ferryboats take people there. Visitors can go up inside Miss Liberty's crown.

Ellis Island is near the Statue of Liberty. From 1892 to 1954, over 17 million people entered the country there. They were given medical tests and asked questions. The Immigration Museum opened on Ellis Island in 1990. Visitors can imagine what the immigrants went through there.

Long Island lies southeast of New York's mainland. New York City's Brooklyn and Queens sections are on the island. So are dozens of small towns.

The Immigration Museum on Ellis Island

The entrance to Ellis Island

The Whaling Museum at Cold Spring Harbor

Walt Whitman was born on Long Island. He wrote *Leaves of Grass*. That is a book of wonderful poems. The Walt Whitman Birthplace can be visited at Huntington. As a boy on Long Island, Whitman loved the sea. The sounds of the sea can be heard in his works.

Whale-watching cruises leave from Long Island. The Whaling Museum is at Cold Spring Harbor. There, visitors learn how whales were once hunted.

EASTERN NEW YORK

Many historic places lie along the Hudson River. Yonkers is on the Hudson just north of New York

City. It is New York's fourth-biggest city. Chemicals and many other goods are made there. Philipse Manor Hall is a famous home in Yonkers. It was built about 1716. Today, it is an art and history museum.

North of Yonkers is the United States Military Academy. It is at West Point. The school is usually called West Point. It is the country's oldest military college. Young people train there to become United States Army officers.

Newburgh is a few miles north of West Point. In 1782-83, Newburgh was George Washington's headquarters. He and Martha Washington lived at the Hasbrouck House. There, visitors can see a desk that Washington used.

Four presidents were born in New York. Three of them grew up near the Hudson River. Theodore Roosevelt was the twenty-sixth president. He was born in New York City. His cousin was Franklin Delano Roosevelt. FDR became the thirty-second president. He was born in Hyde Park. That is not far from Newburgh. His home is called Springwood. FDR had polio. He couldn't walk without help. At Springwood, visitors can see his wheelchair.

President Martin Van Buren was born in Kinderhook. That is north of Hyde Park. Van

West Point cadets

Presidents Ulysses Grant and Dwight Eisenhower were West Point graduates.

Kinderhook is a Dutch word meaning "children's corner."

Ceremonial office room of the New York State Capitol

The State Capitol

Buren's birthplace is gone now. But the thirty-six-room home where he later lived is still standing. The expression "O.K.," meaning "all right," may have come from Van Buren's nickname. The eighth president was called "*Old Kinderhook.*"

Albany lies on the Hudson River northwest of Kinderhook. Albany is one of the country's oldest cities. The Dutch settled it in 1624. It has been New York's capital since 1797. New York's lawmakers meet in the state capitol. It looks something like a castle.

The Schuyler Mansion is in Albany. Philip Schuyler was a Revolutionary War general. His daughter married Alexander Hamilton in that

house. Hamilton was the first United States secretary of the treasury. His picture is on $10 bills.

The New York State Museum is also in Albany. It was founded in 1836. This museum is the oldest and biggest state museum. One display re-creates the Ice Age. It includes life-size models of mother and baby mastodons.

The Baseball Hall of Fame, in Cooperstown

Cooperstown is west of Albany. It is home to the National Baseball Hall of Fame. Great baseball players are honored there.

The Adirondack Mountains are to the northeast. In 1892, most of the Adirondack area became a park. Adirondack Park covers about 9,000 square miles. It is the biggest park in the eastern United States.

Adirondack Park is bigger than the state of Massachusetts.

About 750 miles of hiking trails wind through the Adirondacks. Hundreds of lakes are there, too. They include Lakes Placid, George, and Champlain. The Winter Olympics were held at Lake Placid in 1932 and 1980. People sail and canoe on these lakes. The Adirondacks also attract skiers.

CENTRAL NEW YORK

There are actually more than 1,800 islands in the Thousand Islands.

The St. Lawrence River separates northwestern New York from Canada. The Thousand Islands are close to the river's head. Vacation homes and resorts are on the islands. Boldt Castle is on Heart Island. George Boldt was a hotel owner. He built the castle as a gift for his wife. It has 120 rooms.

Syracuse is about in the middle of New York. It was settled in 1786. Syracuse was named for an ancient Greek city. Today, Syracuse is the state's fifth-largest city. Its Erie Canal Museum shows how the canal was built. The city is also home to Syracuse University.

Southwest of Syracuse is Locke. President Millard Fillmore was born there. The thirteenth

Boldt Castle, on Heart Island

president's log birthplace is gone. One that looks like it was built at Fillmore Glen State Park. That is in nearby Moravia.

To the northwest is Auburn. The Harriet Tubman Home and the William Seward House are there. Tubman was a black woman. She was a famous worker on the Underground Railroad. Tubman helped more than 300 slaves escape. Visitors to her home can see her bed and Bible. Seward was a United States secretary of state. In 1867, he bought Alaska from Russia.

Due west is Seneca Falls. The Elizabeth Cady Stanton Home is there. Visitors can see where the women's rights leader lived. In 1979, the National Women's Hall of Fame opened in Seneca Falls. Great American women are honored there.

To the south is Ithaca. Cornell University was founded there in 1865. The school overlooks Cayuga Lake. Around Ithaca are many waterfalls. Taughannock Falls is the highest waterfall in the northeast. It drops 215 feet.

Farther south is Elmira. Mark Twain spent many summers at Quarry Farm, outside Elmira. There, he wrote parts of *Huckleberry Finn* and *Tom Sawyer*. The study where Twain worked is now at Elmira College.

Taughannock Falls

Mark Twain's study, in Elmira

WESTERN NEW YORK

Corning is northwest of Elmira. The Corning Glass Center is there. Visitors can learn all about glass and glassmaking. Glass objects up to 3,500 years old are displayed there. The Corning Glass Works makes Steuben crystal and other glass objects. It even made a giant 200-inch mirror for California's Mount Palomar telescope.

To the north on Lake Ontario is Rochester. It is the state's third-biggest city. The George Eastman House has a photography museum. It shows how Eastman Kodak makes film.

Margaret Strong of Rochester collected dolls and toys. They can be seen at the Strong Museum. This is a history museum named for her. The Rochester Museum and Science Center has many displays. Visitors can learn about the area's Seneca Indians.

To the southeast on Lake Erie is Buffalo. It is the state's second-biggest city. Canada is just west of Buffalo. Much trade between the United States and Canada goes through Buffalo. Buffalo makes more flour than any other United States city. The city is a railroad center. It is also a port for Lake Erie shipping.

Rochester was named for Nathaniel Rochester, who founded the town in 1812.

A view of the Buffalo skyline from the Erie Basin Marina

44

Buffalo is a great sports town. The Buffalo Bills play pro football there. Buffalo is also home to the Sabres of pro hockey. Children love the Buffalo Zoo. Gorillas, lions, and of course buffaloes can be seen there.

Niagara Falls is a great place to end a New York trip. It is just north of Buffalo. The falls is on the Niagara River. There, the river forms the New York-Canada border. Two falls make up Niagara Falls. American Falls is on the New York side. It has a 176-foot drop. It is about 1,000 feet wide. Horseshoe Falls is on the Canada side. It has a 167-foot drop. Horseshoe Falls is 2,600 feet wide. Few wonders compare to the crashing waters of Niagara Falls.

American Falls, the New York side of Niagara Falls

A Gallery
of Famous
New Yorkers

A GALLERY OF FAMOUS NEW YORKERS

Many New Yorkers have made their marks on the world. They include authors, athletes, and political leaders.

Hiawatha was an Iroquois leader. He lived about 400 years ago. When Hiawatha was young, there was always fighting among the Iroquois. Hiawatha's family was murdered. He was expected to fight back. Instead, he got the five groups of Iroquois to stop fighting. Hiawatha helped set up the Iroquois Federation.

Elizabeth Ann Seton (1774-1821) was born in New York City. Her husband died in 1803. Seton became a Catholic in 1805. She spent the rest of her life doing good deeds. In 1808, she opened a Catholic school in Maryland. This marked the start of the country's Catholic school systems. The next year she founded the Sisters of Charity. This group of women still helps the needy.

Two early American authors were born in New York City. **Washington Irving** (1783-1859) is called the "Father of American Literature." One of his stories is "Rip Van Winkle." It is about a man who slept for twenty years. **Herman Melville**

In 1975, Elizabeth Ann Seton (above) became the first person born in the United States to be declared a saint by the Roman Catholic Church.

Opposite page: Eleanor Roosevelt

47

John D. Rockefeller

Fiorello LaGuardia

(1819-1891) went to sea as a cabin boy in 1839. His great book was *Moby Dick*. It tells about the hunt for a huge whale.

John D. Rockefeller (1839-1937) was born in Richford. He founded the Standard Oil Company in 1870. His wealth grew to over $1 billion. Rockefeller gave much of his money to colleges and churches. His son, **John D. Rockefeller, Jr.** (1874-1960), continued that work. He also built New York City's Rockefeller Center.

Fiorello LaGuardia (1882-1947) was born in New York City. As a boy, LaGuardia learned many languages. He became a translator at Ellis Island. Later, he became mayor of New York City (1934-1945). He improved the city's government. LaGuardia also made health care and housing better for New Yorkers. LaGuardia Airport is named for him.

Eleanor Roosevelt (1884-1962) was born in New York City. She married Franklin D. Roosevelt in 1905. She was a great first lady while FDR was president. She worked to help the poor people of the world. She also represented the United States in the United Nations (1945-1952, 1961-1962).

Bella Abzug (born in 1920), **Shirley Chisholm** (born in 1924), and **Geraldine Ferraro**

(born in 1935) served in Congress. Abzug and Chisholm were born in New York City. Ferraro was born in Newburgh. Abzug gained fame as a foe of nuclear weapons. She also fought for women's rights. Chisholm taught nursery school before entering politics. She became the first black woman in Congress. She was a voice for the poor. Ferraro taught high school and became a lawyer. Then she served in Congress. In 1984, the Democratic Party chose her to run for vice president.

Clara Hale (1905-1992) was born in Pennsylvania. Later, she moved to New York City. Hale raised three children of her own and forty foster children. Then, at age sixty-three, she began car-

Left: Geraldine Ferraro
Right: Shirley Chisholm

Bella Abzug served in Congress from 1971 to 1977. Shirley Chisholm served there from 1969 to 1983. Geraldine Ferraro served from 1978 to 1984.

49

ing for drug-addicted babies. Their mothers were addicts. She founded Hale House in New York City. Hundreds of babies have been nursed back to health there.

Jonas Salk was born in New York City in 1914. He found a way to prevent polio. This disease had crippled many people—including FDR. Starting in 1954, the Salk vaccine was given to millions of children. It has saved countless lives.

Anna Moses (1860-1961) was born in Greenwich. She is known for her paintings of country scenes. Most people called her Grandma Moses. She didn't start painting until she was about eighty. But she painted about 2,000 works.

Grandma Moses

Edward Hopper (1882-1967) was born in Nyack. He is known as the "Painter of Loneliness." His paintings show lonely city scenes. *Nighthawks* is Hopper's best-known work.

George Gershwin (1898-1937) was born in New York City. He wrote many songs. They include "Love Walked In" and "Oh, Lady, Be Good!" Another great composer was Irving Berlin (1888-1989). He was born in Russia. But he lived most of his life in New York City. His songs include "White Christmas," "Easter Parade," and "God Bless America."

Baseball's Lou Gehrig (1903-1941) was born in New York City. He played for his hometown Yankees. Gehrig belted twenty-three career home runs with the bases loaded. This is a record. He also played in a record 2,130 straight games.

*Left: Lou Gehrig
Right: George Gershwin*

Koufax and the Dodgers moved from Brooklyn to Los Angeles, California, in 1958.

Kareem Abdul-Jabbar

Warren Spahn and **Sandy Koufax** were great pitchers. Spahn was born in Buffalo in 1921. He won 363 games. No other pitcher born in the 1900s has won that many. Koufax was born in Brooklyn in 1935. He played for his hometown Dodgers. He threw four no-hitters. Both men are in the Baseball Hall of Fame in Cooperstown.

Kareem Abdul-Jabbar was born in New York City in 1947. He scored 38,387 points in his career. Abdul-Jabbar's "sky hook" helped him set this record.

Woody Allen was born in New York City in 1935. He has written, directed, and acted in many movies. *Annie Hall* and *Bananas* are among the best known. In 1977, he won two Academy Awards for *Annie Hall.* **Jodie Foster** was born in New York City in 1963. She has won two Academy Awards for best actress (1988 and 1991). **Tom Cruise** was born in 1962 in Syracuse. He starred in *Top Gun* and *Rain Man.* **Rod Serling** (1924-1975) was also born in Syracuse. He created "Twilight Zone." It was a famous television show.

Lyman Frank Baum (1856-1919) was born in Chittenango. That is near Syracuse. He wrote *The Wizard of Oz.* **Maurice Sendak** was born in Brooklyn in 1928. His best-known book is *Where*

Maurice Sendak

the Wild Things Are. Sendak did both the pictures and story for that book. **James Baldwin** (1924-1987) was born in New York City. He was a dishwasher before gaining fame as an author. He wrote about what it is like to be black in America. *Nobody Knows My Name* is one of his best-known books.

The birthplace of Maurice Sendak, Grandma Moses, Eleanor Roosevelt, and Shirley Chisholm . . .

Home also to Sojourner Truth, Irving Berlin, Clara Hale, and Lou Gehrig . . .

The site of the Statue of Liberty, the Empire State Building, and Niagara Falls . . .

The top state for making clothing and books . . .

This is New York—the Empire State!

Did You Know?

Smith Brothers cough drops are popular among people with colds. William Wallace Smith and Andrew Smith founded their cough drop business in Poughkeepsie in 1847. Their pictures can be seen on Smith Brothers cough drops boxes.

The Statue of Liberty was created by French sculptor Frédéric Auguste Bartholdi. He modeled the statue's face after his mother's.

Many people call the United States government "Uncle Sam." During the War of 1812 (1812-1815), Sam Wilson opened a meat-packing plant in Troy. Meat shipped by Wilson to the army was stamped "U.S." This stood for United States. But plant workers joked that it stood for "Uncle Sam" Wilson. By 1815, "Uncle Sam" had caught on as a nickname for the government.

One of the country's best baseball card collections is at the Metropolitan Museum of Art. It contains about 16,000 cards. They include the famous Honus Wagner cards, worth hundreds of thousands of dollars.

New York City has about 2,100 bridges—more than any other United States city.

New York has towns named Alabama, Florida, Wyoming, Cuba, Greece, Mexico, Poland, and Peru. Horseheads, Sugar Loaf, Clockville, Painted Post, Chili Center, and Surprise are other New York towns with unusual names.

Charles Feltman is credited with inventing the hot dog about 100 years ago on Coney Island. Every July 4th, Nathan's at Coney Island holds "The Hot Dog Eating Contest." Frank De La Rosa won the 1992 contest. He ate twenty-one hot dogs in twelve minutes.

Long ago, when it thundered, people along the Hudson told their children, "That's just Henry Hudson and his men playing tenpins." The old Dutch game of tenpins became the sport of bowling.

In 1990, Leonard Stellpflug of Rush grew the biggest pumpkin on record. It weighed 821 pounds.

The Dutch named many places in New York. Brooklyn and Harlem are parts of New York City. They were named for Breuckelen and Haarlem in the Netherlands.

George Clinton served as a state governor longer than any other person. He governed New York for twenty-one years (1777-1795 and 1801-1804).

Stuffed animals called teddy bears were named for President Theodore Roosevelt, who was known as "Teddy."

The Dutch people of New York introduced many foods to America. They ate a cabbage salad called *koolsla*. In English, that's cole slaw. They also enjoyed fried cakes called *olykoecks*. They are doughnuts in English.

Marian Donovan, a New York woman, invented the disposable diaper in 1951. It has helped millions of families.

New York Information

State flag

Rose

Maple tree

Area: 49,108 square miles (the thirtieth-biggest state)

Greatest Distance North to South: 307 miles

Greatest Distance East to West: 314 miles

Borders: Canada to the north; Canada, Pennsylvania, and Lakes Ontario and Erie to the west; Pennsylvania and New Jersey to the south; the Atlantic Ocean, Connecticut, Massachusetts, and Vermont to the east

Highest Point: Mount Marcy, 5,344 feet above sea level

Lowest Point: Sea level, along the Atlantic Ocean

Hottest Recorded Temperature: 108° F. (at Troy, on July 22, 1926)

Coldest Recorded Temperature: -52° F. (at Old Forge, on February 18, 1979)

Statehood: The eleventh state, on July 26, 1788

Origin of Name: New York was named for James, the English Duke of York and Albany

Capital: Albany

Counties: 62

United States Representatives: 31 (as of 1992)

State Senators: 61

State Representatives: 150

State Song: "I Love New York," by Steve Karmen

State Motto: *Excelsior* (Latin, meaning "Ever Upward")

Nickname: "Empire State"

State Seal: Adopted 1882

State Flag: Adopted 1909

State Flower: Rose

State Bird: Bluebird

State Tree: Sugar maple

State Animal: Beaver

State Fish: Brook trout

State Insect: Ladybug

State Fruit: Apple   **State Gem:** Garnet

Mountains: Adirondacks, Catskills, Taconics, Shawangunks

Some Rivers: Hudson, St. Lawrence, Mohawk, Delaware, Susquehanna, Genesee, Niagara

Some Waterfalls: Niagara, Taughannock, Buttermilk

Some Lakes: Chautauqua, Oneida, George, Champlain, Erie, Ontario, the Finger Lakes

Some Islands: Long, Manhattan, Staten, Liberty, Ellis, the Thousand Islands

Wildlife: Deer, foxes, porcupines, opossums, skunks, bears, wildcats, muskrats, rabbits, raccoons, woodchucks, beavers, bluebirds, geese, ducks, wild turkeys, falcons, hawks, orioles, woodpeckers, meadowlarks, owls, robins

Manufactured Products: Books, magazines, clothing, cameras, scientific instruments, toys and games, silverware, chemicals, glass, medicines, bread and other foods, jewelry, furniture, paper, pens and pencils, soaps, musical instruments, soft drinks, car parts, computers, many kinds of machinery, lumber

Farm Products: Milk, apples, cherries, grapes, pears, snap beans, lettuce, cabbages, potatoes, sweet corn, onions, maple syrup, plums, strawberries, tomatoes, green peas, hay, dry beans, beef cattle, poultry, eggs

Mining Products: Limestone, sand and gravel, salt, garnet, oil, natural gas, lead, zinc, gypsum

Fishing Products: Lobsters, oysters, clams, scallops, flounder, perch, trout

Population: 17,990,455, second only to California in population (1990 U.S. Census Bureau figures)

Largest Cities (1990 Census):

New York City	7,322,564	Albany	101,082
Buffalo	328,123	Utica	68,637
Rochester	231,636	New Rochelle	67,265
Yonkers	188,082	Mount Vernon	67,153
Syracuse	163,860	Schenectady	65,566

Bluebird

Beaver

Garnet

New York History

9000 B.C.—Ancient Indians reach New York

1300—Iroquois Indians are living in New York

1524—Giovanni da Verrazano is the first European to enter New York

1609—Samuel de Champlain explores New York for France; Henry Hudson explores it for the Netherlands; the area is named New Netherland

1624—The Dutch found New York's first European-built town, Fort Orange (now Albany)

1625—The Dutch start laying out New Amsterdam (now New York City)

1664—England takes control of New Netherland and renames it New York

1690—Schenectady is attacked by French and Indian forces

1763—England defeats France for control of North America

1775—The Americans begin fighting the Revolutionary War

1776—The United States declares its independence from England

1783—In the war's last major action, English forces leave New York City on November 25

1788—New York becomes the eleventh state on July 26

1797—Albany becomes New York's capital

1825—The Erie Canal opens

1827—New York outlaws slavery, freeing about 10,000 slaves in the state

1831—New York's first railroad begins running from Albany to Schenectady

1837—New York native Martin Van Buren becomes the eighth president of the United States

1848—Elizabeth Cady Stanton and Lucretia Mott organize the nation's first women's rights convention at Seneca Falls

The Nielson House at Saratoga National Historical Park, a Revolutionary War site

1850—Millard Fillmore becomes the thirteenth president of the United States

1861-65—Nearly 500,000 New Yorkers help the North win the Civil War

1883—The Brooklyn Bridge is completed

1886—The Statue of Liberty is completed

1901—Theodore Roosevelt becomes the twenty-sixth president of the United States

1917-18—After the United States enters World War I, 518,864 New Yorkers serve; about 14,000 die

1929-39—The Great Depression hits the country

1933—Franklin D. Roosevelt becomes the thirty-second president of the United States

1939—The New York World's Fair opens in New York City

1941-45—After the United States enters World War II, more than 1.6 million New York men and women serve; 31,000 die

1952—United Nations headquarters is completed in New York City

1968—Shirley Chisholm becomes the first black woman elected to the U.S. Congress

1978—People are forced to leave their homes because of toxic waste in the Love Canal neighborhood of Niagara Falls

1984—New Yorker Geraldine Ferraro becomes the first woman to run for vice president for a major party

1988—New York celebrates 200 years of statehood

1989—David Dinkins is elected as New York City's first black mayor

1990—The population of the Empire State reaches 17,990,455

1993—A bomb explosion at the World Trade Center kills 6 people and injures more than 1,000; the storm of the century hits the East Coast, dumping 45 inches of snow on Syracuse in one weekend

The United Nations headquarters

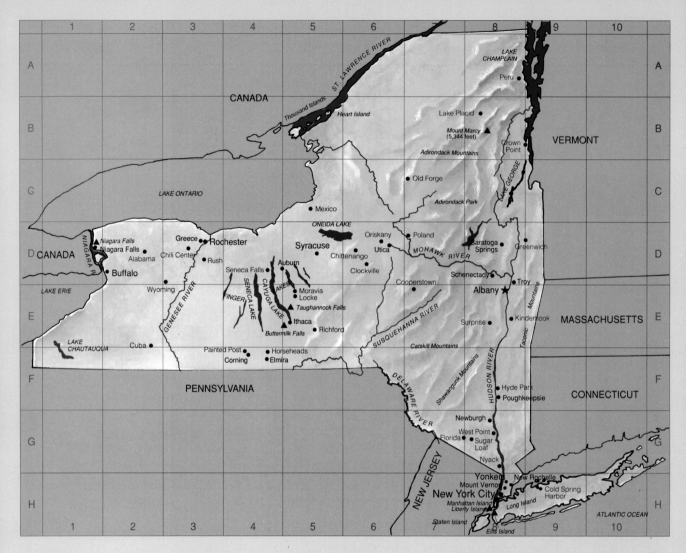

MAP KEY

GLOSSARY

acid rain: Rain that has been polluted by chemicals

ancient: Relating to a long-ago time

antislavery: Against slavery

billion: A thousand million (1,000,000,000)

borough: A section or division of a city

canal: An artificially made waterway that connects two natural bodies of water

capital: A city that is the seat of government

capitol: A building where the government meets

climate: The typical weather of a region

constitution: A framework of government

empire: A powerful people, country, or territory

evacuate: To leave a place

explorer: A person who visits and studies unknown lands

foster children: Children cared for and raised by people who are not their parents

glacier: A mass of slowly moving ice

Hispanic: A person of Spanish-speaking background

hurricane: A huge storm that forms over an ocean, causing great damage to property when it reaches land

independence: Being able to control one's own government

mammoths and mastodons: Prehistoric animals that were much like elephants

manufacturing: The making of products

million: A thousand thousand (1,000,000)

pollute: To make dirty and unsafe for human, animal, or plant life

population: The number of people in a place

slavery: A practice in which people are owned by other people

translator: A person who takes the words of one language and puts them in another

Underground Railroad: A series of hiding places for slaves who were escaping to freedom in Canada

*The Schoharie River,
in the Catskills*

PICTURE ACKNOWLEDGMENTS

Front cover, © Paul Kenward/**Tony Stone Images**; 1, © Doug Armand/**Tony Stone Images**; 2, **Tom Dunnington**; 3, © Paul Meredith/**Tony Stone Images**; 4-5, **Tom Dunnington**; 6-7, © Willard Clay/**Tony Stone Images**; 8, © Dennis O'Clair/**Tony Stone Images**; 9 (left), **© Tom Till**; 9 (right), **courtesy of Hammond, Incorporated, Maplewood, New Jersey**; 10 (top), © Thomas Kitchin/**Tom Stack & Associates**; 10 (bottom), © Peter Cole/**N E Stock Photo**; 11, © Jim Schwabel/**N E Stock Photo**; 12, **© Tom Till**; 15, **Stock Montage, Inc., hand-colored**; 16, **North Wind Picture Archives, hand-colored**; 17, © Jim Schwabel/**N E Stock Photo**; 18, **© James P. Rowan**; 19, **North Wind Picture Archives, hand-colored**; 20, © Jim Schwabel/**N E Stock Photo**; 21 (left), **Sophia Smith Collection, Smith College, Northampton, Massachusetts**; 21 (right), **National Park Service**; 22, **© David Forbert**; 23, **North Wind Picture Archives, hand-colored**; 24 (top), **Stock Montage, Inc.**; 24 (bottom), **AP/Wide World Photos**; 25, © Buddy Mays/**Travel Stock**; 27, © Gala/**SuperStock**; 28, © Don Hamerman/**N E Stock Photo**; 29 (top), © Brent Winebrenner/**mga/Photri, Inc.**; 29 (bottom), **© Cameramann International, Ltd.**; 30 (top), © Don Hamerman/**N E Stock Photo**; 30 (bottom), **© Joan Dunlop**; 31, © Clyde H. Smith/**N E Stock Photo**; 32-33, © David Forbert/**SuperStock**; 34, © Gregory Martin/**SuperStock**; 35 (top), © Sal Maimone/**SuperStock**; 35 (bottom), © David Forbert; 36 (left), © G. L. French/**H. Armstrong Roberts**; 36 (right), © The Photo Source/**SuperStock**; 37 (top), © George Goodwin/**SuperStock**; 37 (bottom), **© David Forbert**; 38, **© David Forbert**; 39, © Kip Brundage/**N E Stock Photo**; 40 (top), © Ralph Krubner/**H. Armstrong Roberts**; 40 (bottom), © David L. Brown/**Tom Stack & Associates**; 41, **© David Forbert**; 42, © David M. Doody/**Tom Stack & Associates**; 43 (top), © Tom Pollak/**SuperStock**; 43 (bottom), © Buddy Mays/**Travel Stock**; 44, James Blank/**Tony Stone Images**; 45, © George Hunter/**SuperStock**; 46, **© The White House Historical Association; photograph by the National Geographic Society**; 47, **Stock Montage, Inc.**; 48 (top), **AP/Wide World Photos**; 48 (bottom), **Stock Montage, Inc.**; 49 (both pictures), **AP/Wide World Photos**; 50, **AP/Wide World Photos**; 51 (both pictures), **AP/Wide World Photos**; 52, **Wide World Photos, Inc.**; 53, **AP/Wide World Photos**; 54 (bottom left), **National Park Service: Statue of Liberty Monument**; 54 (bottom right), **Museum of City of New York**; 54-55 (top), **courtesy of the U.S. Army**; 55 (bottom), **© Carol-Lynn Russel Waugh**; 56 (top), **courtesy Flag Research Center, Winchester, Massachusetts 01890**; 56 (middle), © Paul L. Meyers/**Root Resources**; 56 (bottom), © Ruth A. Smith/**Root Resources**; 57 (top), © Jeremy Woodhouse/**N E Stock Photo**; 57 (middle), © Wendy Shatil/Bob Rozinski/**Tom Stack & Associates**; 57 (bottom), © Louise K. Broman/**Root Resources**; 58, **© Tom Till**; 59, © Grace Schaub/**SuperStock**; 60-61, **Tom Dunnington**; 62, © Augusts Upitis/**SuperStock**; back cover, © Ian J. Adams/**Dembinsky Photo Assoc.**

INDEX

Page numbers in boldface type indicate illustrations.

ABOUT THE AUTHOR

Dennis Brindell Fradin is the author of 150 published children's books. His works for Childrens Press include the Young People's Stories of Our States series, the Disaster! series, and the Thirteen Colonies series. Dennis is married to Judith Bloom Fradin, who taught high-school and college English for many years. She is now Dennis's chief researcher. The Fradins are the parents of two sons, Anthony and Michael, and a daughter, Diana. Dennis graduated from Northwestern University in 1967 with a B.A. in creative writing, and has lived in Evanston, Illinois, since that year.